SYSTEMIC RACISM

AN AMERICAN POETIC ANALYSIS

CARLOS MUHAMMAD

Printed in the United States of America by Kindle Direct Publishing.

Designed and edited by Jovon M. Swan

ISBN 978-0-578-83216-6

PUBLISHING

For my brother *Dedrick A. Muhammad.*

You have always pushed me even at times when I wasn't pushing myself. During times when you were going through your own trials and tribulations you managed to look pass them to tell me to soar.

This is my attempt to make us all soar together. Hopefully, this book will make you proud.

CONTENT

Introduction

Systemic racism is as old and dear to America as apple pie. Sadly, since its inception the very foundation and principals that formed America also formed its tenets. This book comes at a time when America is facing its past and looking at all that she's become in the mirror. The year 2020 was a turbulent year not only because it was a year that America faced tremendous trials due to the Corona Virus (Covid-19) pandemic, but also one where the death of Breonna Taylor and then George Floyd; who died at the hands of police officer Derek Michael Chauvin; brought the ongoing systemic racism pandemic to the surface.

Americans of all walks of life, races, creeds, religious and philosophical persuasions took to the streets in protest and rallies that led to some riots. The sentiments "Black Lives Matter" not only reflected the organization established during the Obama Administration years but were echoed more readily by educational and corporate institutions. The cries for social justice became a theme of importance and America came face to face with the ugly realities that Black people in particular but people of color in general continuously experience.

This book "Systemic Racism: An American Poetic Analysis although written in poetic language and prose serves as my contribution to the topic. In the midst of working on the release of my planned second book of Poetry entitled Pen-spiration: The Dual Nature of the Pen this book due to the climate and some of the time sensitive messages placed that release on the back burner. It is my desire that every line of this book be placed under a microscope, examined, and viewed objectively as another contribution in literature from a great line of Black Writers. It is my objective that this work will be met with critique and consideration that hopefully will create conversation. It is also my desire that everyone reading this book will look at themselves and reflect on where they stand as the topic of Systemic Racism is approached. Are you actively working to build or destroy it? Are you more comfortable seeing others uncomfortable if it infringes on your own privilege or do you share the sentiments of Dr. King that once wrote in his Letter from the Birmingham Jail that:

"Injustice anywhere is a threat to justice everywhere. We are caught in an inescapable network of mutuality, tied in a single garment of destiny. Whatever affects one directly, affects all indirectly."

I want to thank you all in advance for accepting this contribution to this topic and hopefully these words will resonate and serve as fuel for future agents of change.

Enjoy!

If you don't understand white supremacy/racism, everything that you do understand will only confuse you.

-Dr.Neely Fuller Jr.

Poetic Intro: Global White Supremacy

White supremacy is and has been
a global institution
ridding the world of conflict resolution
infiltrating nations
giving birth to privilege
while erecting walls
and creating its own tenets
holding people as tenants
making racism systemic
in nations globally
effecting all the people in it
on it
refusing to own it
disown it
continuing to wear it
while the world continues to perish
breaking,
embracing not burying
the burden
of the brunt
generation after generation
being born to bear it...

CHAPTER 6: THE IMPACT

SWEET POTATO PIE

I want my Sweet Potato Pie
in the sky after I die
so I can meet chubby little white angels
with Kentucky Fried Chicken Wings
walk on cotton made clouds
probably picked by my ancestors
with roads paved in stolen gold
from Africa
with pearly white gates
because everything white is right.
Right?
I don't want to enter a Black Hell
where the son of perdition
or Prince of Darkness dwells
because everything bad
I've ever known was Black.
so why would I want to enter
another place
like that
for eternity
allowing some pitched forked Devil
under the ground
to burn me in his inferno
set aflame
externally
and internally
after being burned on this Earth
since birth
Is there something even worse?

I want my Sweet Potato Pie
in the sky after I die
so I can meet chubby little white angels
with Kentucky Fried Chicken Wings
or is Popeyes a better choice?
Will Jesus provide me with sweet heat sauce
to explain to me that being
sweet in the heat
shows polarity in duality

1

or the middle where Heaven and Hell meet
allowing me to see the sweet face of God
and look at the sweet white face
of Jesus his son,
bearing a striking resemblance
to Cesare Borgia
or a sweet relative of Micheal Angelo
as oppose to being subjected to the heat
I'd face from a dark one?

I asked for my Sweet Potato Pie in the sky
but instead someone gave me a pie
with beans
told me what I've learned was a lie
and started dispelling the myth of my chubby
little white angels
with Kentucky Fried Chicken Wings.
Told me my heaven was right here on Earth
and how I've been manipulated since birth
and how all I've learned in some way,
shape and form
were tenets of global white supremacy
explained to me how racism was systemic
and institutionalized
and not to depend on others because
God was always in me.
Explained to me how racism was finished
and a black inferiority complex
allowed me to depend on others when
God was always in me.

God was always in us.

Time to save ourselves.

NIGGAS AND BITCHES (Jasmin)

All you Niggas just want to be NIGGAS
So guess what, I'm gonna call you niggas...

Everybody wanna be felon niggas
thugged out rebelling niggas
popping pill,
cocaine selling niggas
Takeshi 69 type
"oh I'm telling" niggas.
I'm telling niggas
to love themselves
but they whispering "white"
and yelling "niggas"
Koon ass
Pop Eyes Chicken Sandwhich
slurping on watermelon niggas.
Emasculated
so I put the "male" in niggas
While the next man is flying your "wiz" a kite,
you DMing, IMing, texting and emailing niggas
While your favorite rappers are selling out
They brag about how they out selling niggas,
While they bragging about transporting
that white,
Whites write about how they were sailing
and transporting
when they start selling niggas
Changed your language, culture, God
Got you eating soul food
hog maws, black eyed peas, collard greens
and chitterling
smelling niggas
Clogged up arteries, high blood pressure
Diabetes, short life span
health failing niggas
Now niggas are, what niggas do
Shine, Koon, Hambones, Spear chuckers
Figure who, Jigga boo
Nigga you,

term of endearment niggas
Crack Epidemic chemist,
Victims of Black Wallstreet defeat,

White Supremacy
Systemic
Tuskegee Experiment niggas
Black talk,
"I ain't hearing it" niggas
Black talk
"Nah"
all I'm hearing is niggas.
now let's talk about BITCHES...

Jasmine
has men
and has been
a has been
attracting titties and ass men
and as men
come as men
run in
cumming
and blasting
she has them
outlast them
then pass them
taking all advances
never surpass them
or ask them
for anything
free good time
then cast them
she sexes
fast
make exes fast
to exit fast
not meant to last
she just wants to give up ass

that's her meaning
not demeaning
she's a female demon
scheming for the semen
no screening
much intervening
seeming pleasing
for the evening
and leaving

before
the morning
fleeting
beating concrete
beaming
from sex
"Who's next?"
this nymphos
fiending

from sex
"Who's next?"
this nymphos
fiending

Is Jasmine a dirty bitch
or is she sexually free?
Would this narrative switch
if we were talking about me
or he,
or we
or how we see
women that love sex
but are ill reputed
when the role switches?
All you niggas
that want to be niggas
and call yourself niggas

that do that
are also
the real bitches...

TOXIC

BITCH GET THE FUCK BACK IN THE HOUSE
were the words he screamed from his mouth
while she was walking out the door
with the baby in her hand
abrupt new plan
He came after her
grabbing her violently
The baby opened her eyes silently
looking on
daddies gone
No mommies gone
because daddies gone mad
This topped every argument they had
Bad temper
Anger
She
whimpered
He
whipped her
to wimp her
into shape.

She claimed she needed
a break
He screamed
BITCH I'LL BREAK YOUR JAW
that was all that she could take
Prior to this night
this last fight
he took
her joy
She proclaimed
I'm taking my things
for years he was taking her
things
she couldn't get back
like
Her spirit
Her freedom

He was the provider
so she felt
she would need him
he cried countless times
how he was
sorry and pleaded to her
after she bled
swollen eyes
bleeding
To her
he was the best thing
she ever had
reminded her
of her Dad.

He promised
to get help
She loved him
and continuously forgave him
Although she was constantly sad
she thought
"Maybe
if I have his baby
it would soften up
the crazy
end the threats to
kill himself
if I left him
a baby
maybe
could
actually save me,
save us
more heart ache and grief"
But the pain was compounded
and the countless times
his fist pounded her
the baby cried

loudly
until the baby fell asleep
But
This night was different
daddy was now grabbing at the baby
while mommy was pulling for the baby
until the baby fell
head-first to the concrete.

The baby let out a cry
then blood poured
from her small frame
violently
appearing
to be
looking on
daddies gone
no mommies gone
now babies gone...

and they both stood silently

thinking

What have we done?

LESSEN PLANS

He didn't learn
his lesson
fast enough
He had to puff
Skip class
surpass
the English, Math
and stuff
His lesson
was spent
Smoking
Grass and stuff.
He puffed puffed
the magic
and dragged on
that lethal
hash and stuff
paid half as much
to pop pills,
to pass
increase the BLAST
and stuff
Curriculum disavowed
move silently
while smoking loud
Move violently in a crowd
Disallowed
in class
and
bowed
to no staff
or admin scum
Too dumb
refuse to succumb
to a weak
curriculum
sick of them
Rep where he's from
numb

to a lesson plan
He lessened plans
for lesson
plans
To fail
or fail to plan
just lessens
the
potentially
greater
and makes them
lesser than
No focus on the zig zag zig
but a zig zag cig
this big bad nig
will split a wig
after he take a swig
Ya dig
While digging his own grave
misbehave to fulfill a crave
a slave to Xanex, Percocets, Mollies
and weed
time that he gave
so depraved
There's no progression in lessons when lessons lessens man,
listen for the lesson I'm stressing
unless you
lessen plans

He didn't learn his lesson
fast enough
Hittin licks and such
being slick with chicks
rolling thick with cliques
and such
his lesson was spent
finding vics and such
He avoided classes
to pass on

learning lies,
tricks and such
school scripts
history, politics, and such
Small snips
slave ships
European conflicts
and such
Curriculum disavowed
moved defiantly
while talking proud
more notoriety
when in a crowd
Disallowed
in class
and
bowed
to no staff
or admin scum
they were too dumb
he refused to succumb
to a weak
curriculum
sick of them
Rep where he's from
numb
to a lesson plan
He lessened plans
for lesson
plans
to fail
or fail to plan
just Lessens
the
potentially
greater
and makes them
lesser than
His focus was a bigger theme

not a school styled scene
His aim was green
building a team
where
the end justified the mean
was last seen
digging his own grave
Misbehaved to fulfill a crave
a slave to money, women,
the American dream
time that he gave
would soon pave
a wave of school
to prison pipeline infractions
system of corrections Man
because
he felt there was no progression
with lessons
when those lessons lessened man
the school system

lessons need some addressing
because they

continuously lessen plans.

DISCOMFORT

Don't patronize me with tokens
or provide me with trinkets
to go along to get along
Meanwhile the very system
you created and upheld to
oppress me
and
suppress me
still remains strong.
Don't paint me as a trouble maker
or disillusioned
when I mention "race"
When "race" is the social construct
You created to keep me in my place.

I'm not comfortable with that.

Don't avoid the topic
to feel comfortable
while my discomfort
is never considered
Meanwhile you mention our gains
and progress
while we suffer on so many levels
disproportionately
and equality and equity
for us has not been delivered.
Are you comfortable
in my discomfort?
Is ending systemic racism
something you really want to see
when white supremacy is global
and continues to perpetuate
the differences between you and me?

I'm not comfortable with that.

STRESS LEVELS

I just drove pass two police officers
Please Lord don't let them follow me

How am I doing?

Let me see...

A corona virus pandemic
in the midst of a hostile climate
of inequality
and racism
that's systemic
coupled with an economy
seeing several crashes
while countless riots and rallies are formed
among the masses.

My spirit is so disturbed right now
stress levels
increasing
I feel so perturbed right now
so I guess I'm releasing.

Just got a call
that a friend passed away
from Covid-19
as soon as I hung up the phone
I signed on social media
and watched another Black Man
being shot on the scene
where there was no crime.
JUST AN ARGUMENT
where law enforcement was called
and left him dead.
This happens too many times.
My spirit is so disturbed right now
Stress levels
increasing
I feel so perturbed right now

so I guess I'm releasing.

Left my mask
on my closet counter
that was supposed to counter
Covid
on my way out the door
so I had to turn back
running late for
an appointment now
thoughts in my mind racing
how
after checking my bank account
I couldn't account for
money that was miscounted
when I thought something
had to be discounted
I'm still short for bills
now I know I need more...
instead I feel more

stress

two co-workers were furloughed
this week
so my heart beats
hard in my chest
wondering what could happen
next
perplexed
those two police sirens
are now
going off in back of me.
would I be the next article
riot, rally
would this end with me
becoming
or making history?

My spirit is so disturbed right now
Stress levels
increasing
I feel so perturbed right now
so I guess I'm releasing.

Officer, May I ask why I'm being pulled

over...

" I love America more than any other country in this world, and, exactly for this reason, I insist on the right to criticize her perpetually. **"**

-James Baldwin

6:PILE OF TRICKS

FECAL MATTERS

Fuck you and your
TRUMP card,
I'll stomp hard on your bullshit.
SHIT...
I never made a BUSH a hero,
alive or dead
condolences zero
but you niggas keep condoning shit
even if their skins like yours
but the allegiance isn't
why are you still owning shit?
I never HAD a President
never claimed one
name one
I remained reluctant or hesitant,
observed how they all functioned
and remained a warner
not one of these mother fuckers
was in our corner.

Even when Bill was the head of state,
and to him
Monica's head was great
He wanted your head
on a stake,
supported by his wife
with the Biden bill
to push mass incarceration
for niggas,
locking our Black asses up
compared to others
at a disproportionate rate
Now Donald Chump says
let's make America great...
again.
What's the real message
he's trying to send?

These are FECAL MATTERS,

ahhh shit
It's all shit
we need to talk about
Let's talk shit out.

Abraham Lincoln had an agenda,
JFK had an agenda
every President gave two fucks about you
Actually no fucks
You just keep getting shitted on
by the RED, WHITE and BLUE.

Wait, the RED
Was colonized by the WHITE
for the BLUE lives to matter.
Matter fact
they keep bending over
opening up their shit hole
to continuously release
fecal matters.
Now it doesn't matter if
the chit chatter hits
national or international
you're still getting brutalized
and battered with
night clubs
outside of a night club
or gunned down
being a catalyst
for movement
that keeps you stagnated
organized marches,
boycotts
but little
to no improvement.

Now you're not drinking Starbucks
Shucks
Do you think they give two fucks?

You'll just run your Black ass
to another one
of their establishments
and they'll still
get the bucks
line their ducks
watch you cowardly chickens
boycott and cluck
what
the fuck
Shut
nothing down
they'll issue an apology
regain your trust
and sympathy
and to them
you'll still remain
the clown
wanting to be down...

These are FECAL MATTERS,
ahhh shit
It's all shit
we need to talk about
Let's talk shit out.

The Clinton's had an agenda,
Barack Obama had an agenda
every President
gave two fucks about you
Actually no fucks
you just keep getting shitted on
by the RED, WHITE and BLUE.

Wait, your RED blood keeps getting shed
to uphold WHITE supremacy
and you're feeling BLUE.
Clearly Black Lives
never mattered

It's fecal
What matters
is the shit they say is true
So their narrative
becomes imperative
Your reason
becomes their treason
Speaking against injustice
makes you Anti-American
Yet, they have you justifying
nigga killing season
SHIT...
You become an opponent
when
you don't condone it
If you support independent Black Leaders
or movements
like South Africans
seizure of land
from white farmers
that originally stole land
from native South Africans
You're told to condemn
and disown it
SHIT...

Nah fuck that shit
I know for you it's
a hard pill to swallow
but I'll continue to clench my black fist
wanting Africans
at home and abroad
to stand high like Killamanjaro
praying and working
for the removal
of all kinds of sorrow
I had to hurry
and get this out
without approval

because in two hours
the content will be old
And there will be more fecal matters
by tomorrow.

Ahhh shit...

MASK

There's a global pandemic,
right?
or maybe I'm crazy
to ask
or take these media outlets
and politicians to task
When they've always been wearing a mask.

Bring out the cast
the worlds a stage
the worlds enraged
The truth becomes the first casualty
where the public is popping a pill
for a placebo of evil,
patented,
purchased
to plague
with Covid-19
A strain of the Corona Virus
emerges on the scene
for new life lessons
shedding light through the iris
giving us
2020 vision
to expand what all these pupils
have seen.
Quarantine
Isolation
to create
eye
Soul
lation
killing local motion
And in the midst of this
Police cause more
racial commotion
always on Blacks Backs
now applying pressure on our necks
over consumed with fear

making us choke on
what we ATE
which was enough FOR SIX

literally taking our last breath
already finding it
difficult to breathe
from wearing this mask.

I'm suffocating
I can't breathe, I can't breathe...

Yet I'm required to wear this mask
during this global pandemic,
right?
or maybe I'm crazy
to ask
or take these police officers
and white corporations
that suddenly realize that
Black Lives Matter to task
When we've provided our service,
bloodshed,
tears and consumer dollars
for a thank you
and a fake smile
because you've always
been wearing your mask.
bring out the cast
better yet the casket
It's becoming more difficult
for you to keep up this
racket
racial
poker facial
facade
after experiencing your mistreatment
for over 400 years
now it's more difficult

to mask it
We see you
faster than 5G
radiation,
because what you radiate
shuns all the hate
you attempted to legislate
from you passing a BILL
to open the GATES

It's becoming more convincing
that we need social distancing
Separation
Six feet away
you engaged in
a six thousand year melee
with us globally
not seeing you properly
so collectively
we were our own delay
to progress
outnumbering you
eleven to one
while going through
a rigorous
rather ridiculous
process
not reading you right
while
repeatedly
receiving receipts
confirmation
that we can no longer
comply and concede
while you obviously
feel obsolete
YOU ARE
the real minority
using the majority

to make you feel complete
while you continuously beat
on us
we stay in this toxic relationship
romancing you
receiving
occasional
trinkets and treats
for trust
illusions of inclusion
a Governor
Mayor
or even a Black President
or Vice-President

that doesn't stop
you from putting your
oppressive
Iron feet on us
still releasing
law Enforcement
and judges
that replaced black robes
and police uniforms
for their white
hoodies and sheets
on us
this can't last
while we try to rationalize
You're busying rationing
out your lies
while protestors
riot, rally
and hit the streets
and others galvanize
to cast
votes
working to Trump
those mistakes from the past

while some want to lull
us further asleep
but many of us keep one eye open
to peep
but
Alas
your own lies and deceit is
removing your mask...

F*CK EM BOTH

Due to this current political climate
I'll create content
about candidates with campaigns
I haven't complied with yet
Everyone's talking about voting
quoting questionable characters
I still haven't aligned with yet.
Instead I'll let my fist pump
showing my own BLACK POWER
bring it down on the heads of
Biden and President Trump
F*CK EM BOTH.

Now if you f*ck with one or BOTH,
that's your prerogative
but don't tell me my
ancestors died
to place in power
the same people
that didn't provide them
with the same supplies to live.
Oh it's about the ancestors
yet you're wearing
those that enslaved your ancestor's
last names
embracing their religion,
culture and God
and acting like
my refusal to give them my vote
is the only thing that will dishonor
and bring the ancestors shame.
Yea I said it F*CK EM BOTH.

Biden spent 47 years in politics
put pen to paper
to produce a crime bill
pushed it to another partner in crime,
Bill
knowing that depressed

and deprived
communities
are more likely to succumb to crime til
they fill
up prisons in large numbers
massively incarcerating Black Males
and many haven't recovered
due to their harsh sentencing
of crimes still
Yet still like the good slave
we run around and defend his honor
and expunge him from his past bad record
while those black males take those conviction
records with them to the grave.
Biden is a changed man we say,
in his past he befriended segregationist,
yet today some things reported about his past were lies
he was doing his job to protect his own
from the same predators
that were "super"
that Hillary despised
Now today he loves Black People
even tossed in a token to tally votes
my disdain for him, is not support for Trump
with conviction I say F*CK EM BOTH.

Now everybody wants to dump Trump
while this country is going down
in the dumps
Trump
is proving that he's a wicked guy
declaring to be the nonpolitical
presidential
President
presenting
inconsequential comments
and evidence
showing his incompetence
can't even allow him and Pence

to keep shit fly.
Rewind to the Central Park Five
where his bias and racism bore its ugly head
five innocent boys convicted of a crime
they didn't commit
and Trump takes out several ads
saying they deserve to be dead.
They are later exonerated
but Trump refuses to apologize.
Yet he says he's the "least" racist
But in our presence he tells the most lies.

Building walls to keep out Mexicans
aren't as big as the walls
he built to separate Americans
not even adequately addressing
the Corona Virus Pandemic
and lost of lives
due to his own ego and arrogance.
Yet still so many of or preachers and pastors
ran to the pulpit for him and prostituted
If your vote is your voice
and America hasn't heard you for over 400 years
I guess your voice has been muted.
Now we stand in the valley of decision
picking the "lessor of two evils"
as an idiom for idiots we quote.
I'll sit this one out and
exercise my freedom of speech
and proudly say F*CK EM BOTH.

ASE'

Oludumere
Please forgive us
for the spirit of our ancestors
that's forgotten
until an election year
where no votes evokes
ancestral anger
putting countless lives in danger

Lord have mercy
for these benevolent white gods
to have mercy
because our lives depend on them
our knees we bend on them
as prey
while we pray
they're scheming
release the Orisha
Yewa
Yemojya bless us with Oya
from your union with Obatala
some of our ancestors called on
Allah Subhanahu Wa Ta'ala
enveloped by the spirit of Oshun
Ogun
while I embodied the spirit of Shango
to mangle these political demons.

Please forgive me...

Have I provoked your ancestral anger
by not lifting up political white men?
Putting my people in danger
by withholding
my vote
refusing to cast?
Was this something that can't be forgiven I ask
or was my vote the most important thing
to remove the ancestor's wrath?

I pray while I'm prey
embody the spirit of Gabriel Prosser,
Denmark Vessey and Nat Turner
on this very day
Sankofa
lit up an incense
sat on the sofa
sipping sweet nectar
with honey not soda
spirit to invoke a riot
I can't deny it one iota
but I approach a racial pandemic
that's systemic
unlike the Corona
hone
a
poetic spirit like Apollo
Or Ausar planting seeds to produce Heru
resurrection of Langston Hughes
with the mind of Frantz Fanon
allowing me to see you
and see through
these uncertain times
and refusing to endorse leadership
that continue to enslave our minds.

Please forgive me...

Have I upset the ancestors
by not voting for the children
of my ancestor's captors
that are in a white privileged position of power
maintaining the same structure
that was created by slave masters.
now you modern day slave bastards
want to cut me off
because of my disrespect of the ancestors
Oh Oludemere
Some say

Allahu Akbar
travels through me
through my DNA
waiting for the lord's vengeance
I just need the word
not a sentence
so I watch
As well as pray
as I see so
many men play
themselves
not recognizing they're Godly Giants
Saying nothing I say is valid
without a ballot
so a damn vote is their only
form of defiance
with white men as their mouthpiece
reducing them down to elves
never realizing
that the energy they're
using they could be
galvanizing
Nation building
and enterprising
as a collective
which is more effective
instead of waiting every four years
to become voting activist
further
pushing an illusion of inclusion
What kind of act is this?
I'm sure the ancestors
wanted more
I Implore
is this what they died for?

Ase'

RACIAL JUNGLE

Animalistic
racial hatred
cannibalistic
Mankind eating man
A kind of man
making some kind of plan
to rule all kinds of land
inhabited by people of color
with no kind of plan
so he rules them
fools them
with some kind of demand
gives them some kind of hand
after having them hand over
their resources,
natural and human
and continuously taking their land over
Colonization
Imperialism,
cultural bandit
what was once yours
was a part of his plan
so stand over
there.

Global warfare

Wanting all of that land
over there
give me a hand over there
join my army
so I can continue to pillage the planet
placing democracy and my plan
over there
give you an opportunity
to come under me
making you feel closer
never becoming my opponent
so we can build a bigger and better

cultural
racial
very inclusive
scary
illusionary world
where you're still a tenant
and I own it
leaving you a small remnant
of what was yours
but I own it
making you feel
you're making progress
while I'm still ten steps ahead of you
so I'm on it
I'm the Tarzan
in this racial jungle
and you all are animals
never capable
of being an equal
with shared rulership
because I won't condone it.

ANOTHER WIN

Another win
for white men
is no cause for us to celebrate
Inserting a token mate
in place with him
doesn't eliminate systemic hate
and racism
symbols without substance
doesn't remove the discussion
It simply adds a black face
to keep the systems in place with them

We yell defund the Police
they put more money in place with them
We scream "it's only my wallet"
and end up with a bullet in our backs
from a high-speed chase with them
knee on our neck,
a severed spine in our back
shot in front of our families
or right in the face with them
end up doing more time
for a crime
as our white counterparts
in a case with them
end up profiled in a store
neighborhoods
in front of our house
when we share the same space with them
I can go on and on
with countless cases
how systemic racism
never ends
and repeat again
and again and again
that
Biden's America
is the same as
Trump's America

Which was the same as
Obama's America
which was no different from
The Bushes and Clinton's America

so for us
there's countless losses
but for them
it's Another Win.

"No matter how big a nation is, it is no stronger than its weakest people, and as long as you keep a person down, some part of you has to be down there to hold him down, so it means you cannot soar as you might otherwise."

-Marian Anderson

CHAPTER 6: THE CHANGE

SYSTEMIC RACISM

It's the subtle racism
that's the blatant racism
sometimes we place
what's in our face
as a safe space
to replace wisdom
Demonizing those that make
A case to deface
what's racism
as the racist
that we face
when the systems laced
with racism

If you celebrate Columbus Day
that's systemic racism
Thanksgiving and Presidents Day
are systemic racism
to a white Jesus you pray
that's systemic racism
all these slogans are so cliche
in our face "E-racism"

Institutionalize the lies
when the racism lies inside
of the lies upheld with pride
for the ties we seldom hide
Racism is not simply actions
but adding actions
are just a fraction
of negative thoughts we multiply
to divide people
and make subtractions
There's inequality
because nobody's equal
we're all just variables
that come up later
with the probability
that

white supremacy is the
common denominator.

If you celebrate Independence Day
that's systemic racism
giving George Washington a Holiday
is systemic racism
the names on streets and buildings today
are systemic racism
all these slogans are so "cliche"
in our face "E-racism"

Red people were colonized
by white people and now they're blue
put the colors in their flag
but never flagged the things they did or do
set up race as a social construct
and made everything about them positive
mistreatment soon followed from attitudes
now embedded in the environment we live
these attitudes formed into beliefs
that hardened into laws
and til this day people
are racially profiled and mistreated
without probable cause
some may argue
that the things I mentioned
shouldn't even have been stated
not realizing systems
continue by the lies perpetuated.

If you subscribe to American History books
that's systemic racism
not realizing the land was stolen by crooks
forming systemic racism
white privilege
from the white power structure today
forms systemic racism
all these slogans are so "cliche"

in our face "E-racism"

NOW...

WE ARE STILL HERE

After you came to take us

you did everything to make us
subservient slaves
Willie lynched us
until we no longer resembled
the proud people we were
became very fearful
and only on occasion
brave
enough to challenge you
refusing to challenge ourselves
you whipped us
beat us
castrated us
still needed us
today you still
repudiate our leaders
to lead us

back then
when we attempted to escape
you did public exhibitions
that were executions
to show others
you can defeat us
and placed our dismembered body parts
in jars on your shelves.
Today however is a new day
so let me make this clear
after all that you've done to us
we are still here.

When we attempted to enterprise
and monopolize

you destroyed our Rosewoods
and Black Wall Streets.
when we worked to create our
own businesses
and HBCU's

you made sure our resources
were limited and our ventures
weren't as competitive and complete
when we worked hard to progress
and move into equal housing
you set up redlining to make
projects and ghettos
our only retreat
when we established our
own organizations
to fight against injustice
you set up Cointelpro
to destroy them
and make them obsolete
then you flooded our neighborhoods
with drugs and guns
after miseducating us
and helping to ensure our dysfunction
knowing people would naturally
become products of environments
that are hostile
and they'd aid in their own self-destruction.
You'd send your police officers
in our neighborhoods
with the aim to kill and justify it
by claiming fear
today however is a new day
so let me make this clear
after all that you've done to us
We are still here.

We are still here
strong and resilient
a mighty people that defeat all the odds
We are still here
Despite what you've done
Because we're still powerful
children of God
Not yet defeated...

ILLITERATION

Topic:
Social Media Discussion On Race

Thoughts:
I'm having trouble
reading
and
reviewing
real
repulsive
repugnant
redundant
ridiculous
rather
racist
rants
with reckless
responses
repetitiously
or am I repeatedly
receiving them
wrongfully?

Am I viewing things
awfully?
or am I really
restraining
rage
while reading
these
reckless
rebuttals
rapidly
wrapping
my mind around
this
artificial
archaic

arrogance
argumentatively
articulating
arbitrary
irrelevant
arguments
so artistically
and arduously
while arranging
their thoughts
with errant
erroneous
erratic
errors
in information
without research
but still relentlessly
wrestling with words
for a win
when warring
with
weak
wicked ways
waywardly
way within
so I sit
succinctly
savagely
seeking
success on the subject
and distressingly
desiring
to strip
these
strangers to
shreds
leaving
strands
stand my ground

to make them
stray away
strong-fully?
Although I know it's
strangely and
strategically
structural
it shouldn't be
stressfully
stress for me
so instead I log off
instead of letting them
emotionally
get the best of me
longingly
languishing
left a few harsh words
laughingly
leaving no room
for
lackluster
language
lacking
luster
refusing to
utter and
muster
another word
so they heard the
last from me.

I'm done...

KAREN'S OBSESSION

There was something about

high concentrations of melanin

that was unsettling

threatening

kept her meddling

questioning in a manner

not very welcoming

emotionally

embellishing

"Why are you here?"

she would ask

the

fledgling

new residents

with no hesitance

her unsolicited

presence

new drama

was now developing

playing fields never leveling

due to privilege

perceived power

and pompous

peddling

her peoples

prominence

prevailed

until people of color

became irrelevant

propelled for awhile

empowered Karen

stayed on the prowl

regularly racially profiled

kept police numbers

on speed dial

see dark skin

she's instantly riled

became vile

played victim while

police pulled up

real hostile

and the innocent negro

ends up on trial

either shot down

or defiled

Emmet Tilled

feeling

all

Pervis's

Payne now

not enough time to be agile

and Karen walks off with a smile.

HOPE

While we helplessly
hope
hope seems to help
with coping
and sorrow
so we hope for healing
hope to be heard
hope for a better tomorrow.

We hope to thrive
hope to survive
hope even
to keep hope alive
hope things get better
hope things are fine
hope that
hope is not just something
in our minds
generations later
we hope
they'll define
a new people that
won't hope forever
because forever seems like such a long time
to hope.

THE LETTER

Dear Sanaa,
I wanted a world that was better for you
so I'm writing this letter for you
my little Black girl
the descendant of greatness
although our people
may debate this
and self hatred
seemed to replace this
but it's true.
I wanted a world that was better for you.

I didn't want you to grow up in a world
marred with inequities
and economic
and racial disparities
educational centers
denying us of our Black Inventors
Scientist
Historians
Kings and Queens
seeing your people in a position
of real authority
not as the first this or the first that
in relation to those showing superiority
reducing us to minorities
embracing inferiority
but displaying that we could be anything
we put our minds to
I wanted a world that was better for you.

I didn't want you to grow up in a world
where
Karen was only caring
to see Black bodies hauled off in body bags
or police cars.
Where Black Women were the most neglected
and disrespected

and molestation cases
weren't reminiscent of our raped ancestors
on the plantation in the big house bearing
the least scars.
I guess covering up wounds
replacing them with accolades
and symbols of success and progress
Isn't supposed to hurt too?
Nah,
I wanted a world that was better for you.

I didn't want you to grow up in a world
where riots and rallies
were responses to injustices
where the outcome increases
more potential violence
from hate groups
comfortable perpetuating
hate practices
Where all of our efforts
seem effortless
Where an incredulous
expression
of progression
of a residential preference
Is met with redlining
and a racial reference
from a banker
not remotely interested
in togetherness
but we must weather this
Storm
normalized conditions
in the disunited states
of America
where a so-called union
was formed
But that union was formed

against us clearly.
So as I conclude this letter
I need you to be much better
than me
Promise me one thing that you will be
and that's a change agent in the kind of world I always wanted to see.

Love,
Your Dad

POETIC OUTRO: SOAR

The sky is open
the universe is expansive
so many possibilities exist
when we can soar.
See ourselves as more
see light through darkness
see a better tomorrow
even while our tears pour.
Soar like an eagle
Soar like a plane
Soar like thought traveling through
dimensions never yet obtained
Soar above the madness
when the world tries to hold you down
explore
those greater heights within yourself and just soar.

In you there's so much greatness
even despite what others see
the ills of systemic racism
could never define what's inside
you and me
There's brilliance in resilience
possibilities still waiting for
a great people
that can see themselves soar.
Soar like a sparrow
Soar to different domains
Soar outside the space within yourself
telling you there's nothing you can gain
Soar and except access
It's really you you've been waiting for
theres so much greatness if you can see yourself soar.

Soar like an eagle
Soar like a plane
Soar like thought traveling through
dimensions never yet obtained

Soar above the madness
when the world tries to hold you down
explore
those greater heights within yourself and just soar.

SYSTEMIC RACISM

RACISM

REFLECTION SESSIONS

Now That you've read the entire book the following pages are geared to make you reflect on what you've read. Please use these activities as a guide for self-reflection and assessment. In addition add them to the discussion in community organization meetings, your book clubs, classrooms and use them as professional development tools at work as you discuss implicit bias, diversity and systemic racism. Please present this topic candidly, honestly and openly. Nothing changes when topics of this magnitude are approached with caution or trepidation. Please be honest regardless to how painful the topic may be.

REFLECTION SESSION #1
The Impact

1. Why is chapter 6 called The Impact?

_____

_____

_____

_____

_____

_____

2. While some poems are explicitly evident in confronting the theme of the book Systemic Racism how does the poems Sweet Potato Pie, Niggas and Bitches, Toxic and Lessen Plans tie into the overall theme? Explain the function of each poem as it relates to the impact of systemic racism.

_____

_____

_____

_____

_____

3. Racism is trauma. Psychologists have determined that racism contributes to bad health, fear, anxiety and post-traumatic stress symptoms. How are those factors mentioned presented in the poem Stress Levels? What other issues does the poem present?.

_____

_____

_____

_____

_____

REFLECTION SESSION #2
Pile of Tricks

1. How does the politics discussed in chapter 6 entitled Pile of Tricks contribute to systemic racism? How have politicians, law enforcement, the judicial system and other institutions contributed to it?

_____

_____

_____

_____

_____

_____

2. How did the Covid-19 pandemic and the health disparities of 2020 between Blacks and Whites in America help to bring the topic of Systemic Racism to the forefront? What poems reflected that racial climate the most? Why?

_____

_____

_____

_____

_____

_____

3. What can politicians do to effectively rid America and the world of Systemic Racism? What can you do to help eliminate global white supremacy and sytemic racism? Can anything actually be done? Reflect and discuss this honestly and candidly.

_____

_____

_____

_____

_____

_____

REFLECTION SESSION #3
The Change

1. The Most Honorable Elijah Muhammad was known for saying you can't change the condition of a people until you can change their thinking. In chapter 6 entitled The Change the poem called Systemic Racism attacks holidays, historic figures, the educational school system as well as infrastructures (to name a few). The poem explicitly states that all of those subjects mentioned contributes to Systemic Racism. How? Please reread the poem to identify everything that was mentioned as contributors to Systemic Racism. Explain your answer.

_____

_____

_____

_____

_____

_____

2. The poem We Are Still Here details many of the challenges that the Black Community faces in America but remain resilient. How important is resilience when it comes to survival in an environment that continues to set up obstacles, bariers and resistance? What are some of the things we can actively do to eliminate those obstacles?

_____

_____

_____

_____

_____

_____

3. In the poem The Letter a promise is requested, what is it? Although the promise was a request for Sanaa, what can you do personally to fulfill that promise? What can we do? Discuss this and create action steps toward fulfilling your part in making the promise a reality.

_____

_____

_____

_____

_____

_____

HOMEWORK

Re-read this book again and pass it on. If these words resonate with you in any way, allow them to serve as fuel for you to do your part in confronting Systemic Racism. Let's put an end to this chapter so that future generations can start a new one.

NOTES

NOTES

NOTES

NOTES

NOTES

NOTES

NOTES

NOTES

NOTES

NOTES

NOTES

ACKNOWLEDGEMENTS

I would like to thank GOD first and foremost for caring enough about Black People in particular and people of color in general and our struggle in America to intervene in our affairs by raising up in our midst the Exalted Christ and providing us with a Grace and Reminder. The entire world will soon know who they are as the world will know and understand who we are and watch us soar.

I would like to thank the ancestors for granting me permission to manifest their ever-present energy, ever living spirit and allowing me to be a vehicle to present this topic in a palatable poetic way. ASE'

I would like to thank all freedom fighters, activists, community organizations as well as religious and educational institutions. Addressing systemic racism at the root and not the surface is the only way to begin to tear down institutions that are literally destroying the moral fiber of this country. The time for sugar coating is over. We are the change we're waiting for.

I would like to thank my Luv4self Publishing/Enterprises family, Dedrick Muhammad and Keith Muhammad. You both have been with me throughout this entire time from Caressed Spirits to Your Daddy Wasn't Sh*t So You're Not Going To Be Sh*T: Removing the harmful effects of curse words. You have stood with me when I was up and when I was down, when I was motivated and not so motivated and for that I can never be appreciative enough.

I would like to thank Krystle Patrick for blessing me with my heart beat and my joy Sanaa Fatirah Muhammad. Regardless to whom or what we will always be family.

This project would not even be possible without the assistance of Jovan Swan who blessed me with editing, formatting, and cover design. I am eternally grateful to you and very appreciative. I am indebted to you. Thank you, thank you, thank you.

To my Mother Grace Glover. I will say what I said in Caressed Spirits and that's "MUCH". To David, Natasha and all of my nieces and nephews, Ayana, Qamara, Qur'an, Mackenzie and D'Khari, you all are up next. Continue to make us proud. To my little brother Darius Glover, when you recognize your power you can rise above everything...Soar. To my cousins Sirod, Dichiara, Jaylin, Dionte and Taylor thanks for always being supportive. To my Aunts and uncles, Mary, Susie, Julia, William, and Lonnie Joe. Aunt Viola and family, Aunt Sadie Mae, and family and all of Aunt Josephine's offspring and our entire family in Chicago, Alabama, Milwaukee and everywhere else I love you.

In loving memory of my Grandmother and Grandfather, Mary and Joseph Huggins and my sister/cousin Kenyetta Hamilton. You are all still living through us.

To my entire North Avenue Connections family (too many to mention) stay tuned for that project.

I could literally go on forever naming and acknowledging people that have impacted me over the years. Your name not being mentioned is not because you're not appreciated but simply because time and space will not permit it. Please charge this one to my head and not my heart. I love you all for your continued prayers, encouragement, and support. I hope you all have enjoyed this book but more importantly I hope you all were encouraged to become change agents.

Thank you all.

OTHER BOOKS BY CARLOS MUHAMMAD

CARESSED SPIRITS:
Poetic Thoughts and Reflections from a Black Man's Perspective

YOUR DADDY WASN'T SH*T, SO YOU'RE NOT GOING TO BE SH*T:
Removing the Harmful Effects of Curse Words

Made in United States
Orlando, FL
07 September 2022

22124680R00057